Trial BY ICE

Trial BY

ICE

A Photobiography of Sir Ernest Shackleton

By K. M. Kostyal

NATIONAL GEOGRAPHIC SOCIETY

Washington, D.C.

*To my father,
Richard, who
loves the sea
and a good
adventure.*

Published by the
National Geographic Society
1145 17th St. N.W.
Washington, D.C. 20036

John M. Fahey, Jr.
*President and Chief Executive
Officer*

Gilbert M. Grosvenor
Chairman of the Board

Nina D. Hoffman
Senior Vice President

William R. Gray
*Vice President & Director
of the Book Division*

Staff for this book:

Nancy Laties Feresten
Director of Children's Publishing

Suzanne Patrick Fonda
Editor

Jennifer Emmett
Assistant Editor

Marianne Koszorus
Art Director

David M. Seager
Designer

Annie Griffiths Belt
Illustrations Editor

Meredith C. Wilcox
Illustrations Coordinator

Carl Mehler
Director of Maps

Joseph F. Ochlak, Michelle H.
Picard, Tibor G. Tóth, Gregory
Ugiansky
Map Research and Production

Elisabeth B. Booz
Researcher

Connie D. Binder
Indexer

Vincent P. Ryan
Manufacturing Manager

Richard S. Wain
Production Manager

*The National Geographic Society gratefully acknowledges the kind
assistance of Valerie Mattingley and Heather Yule of the Society's
United Kingdom office, and Cary Wolinsky.*

Library of Congress Cataloging-in-Publication Data
Kostyal, K. M., 1951–
          Trial by ice : a photobiography of Sir Ernest Shackleton /
by K. M. Kostyal
                              p.   cm.
          Summary: Traces the adventurous life of the South Pole explorer
whose ship, the *Endurance,* was frozen in ice and crushed, leaving the captain
and crew to fight for survival.
          ISBN 0–7922–7393–1
          1. Shackleton, Ernest Henry, Sir, 1874–1922 Juvenile literature.
2. Explorers—Great Britain Biography Juvenile literature. 3. Antarctica—
Discovery and exploration Juvenile literature. 4. Shackleton, Ernest Henry, Sir,
1874–1922 Pictorial works Juvenile literature. 5. Explorers—Great Britain
Pictorial works Juvenile literature. 6. Antarctica—Discovery and exploration
Pictorial works Juvenile literature. [1. Shackleton, Ernest Henry, Sir,
1874–1922. 2. Explorers. 3. Antarctica—Discovery and exploration.]   I. Title.
G875.S5K67   1999
919.8'904—dc21   99-20980

Printed in the United States of America

*Dust jacket: (front) Sir Ernest Shackleton is inset against an Antarctic background
showing the* Endurance *held fast in ice; (back) sled dogs watch as their former home
disintegrates. Front cover: A foil stamp shows a stylized rendering of* Endurance
*silhouetted against an iceberg. Title page: Sculptures of nature, giant icebergs sail
on the winds and currents of Antarctic seas.*

"I dreamt...that some day I would go to the region of ice and snow and go on and on till I came to one of the poles of the earth, the end of the axis upon which this great ball turns."

Alexandra Shackleton examines the Bible her grandfather carried to Antarctica, her face reflected on his portrait.

FOREWORD

"ARE YOU RELATED TO THE ANTARCTIC EXPLORER ERNEST SHACKLETON?" Since childhood, I have been asked that question. My father, Edward, was Ernest Shackleton's younger son, and I cannot remember a time when I was not aware of the part the great white continent had played in the life of my family.

Photographs from my grandfather's expeditions hung on the walls at home: beautiful black-and-white images from the early years of the century. They showed a world of snow and ice; bearded men in strange, shapeless garments; a little ship being slowly crushed in the ice, her decline more shocking in each photograph until she is finally only a skeleton of a ship. As a child, I was always particularly fascinated by one photograph. It showed the huskies (the sled dogs) sitting patiently on the ice beside the wreck of the ship that had been their home, her end not far away, their future in doubt.

Ernest Shackleton died at the start of his third expedition. He was only 47. My father was nine years old. He did not have the chance to know his father very well (explorers were away for years at a time then), yet he, too, became an explorer. At the age of 20 he went to Borneo and then to Ellesmere Island in the Canadian Arctic. He avoided the Antarctic because he did not want to seem to be trading on his father's name. When I was a little girl, I remember sitting on the coalhouse roof with my brother one day, pretending it was a ship. I made him promise that he, too, would explore, to make it three generations. And he did. He took part in an expedition to Devon Island, in the Canadian Arctic.

I did get to the Antarctic, nearly a hundred years after my grandfather, on a naval ship bearing the same name as his ship— *Endurance.* It was only a small glimpse of the Antarctic he had known, but it was an unforgettable experience. Perhaps after reading this excellent book, some of you too will be inspired to visit the great white south in the footsteps of Sir Ernest Shackleton.

Alexandra Shackleton

"The cliffs are of a dazzling whiteness, with wonderful blue shadows. Far inland higher slopes can be seen, appearing like dim blue or faint golden fleecy clouds."

THE WILD FROZEN BEAUTY OF ANTARCTICA WAS A LONG WAY FROM THE gentle green hills of Ireland's County Kildare, where Ernest Henry Shackleton was born. At his birth in 1874 no one could have imagined that this baby would grow up to be one of the world's greatest Antarctic explorers. In fact, it's doubtful that anyone in Ireland gave much thought to the southern continent at the end of the Earth.

The world of Ernest's early childhood was simple. People still traveled by horse and buggy, and there were no airplanes or telephones. An old castle topped a hill near the Shackleton family's rambling house, and country lanes crisscrossed the area's endless potato fields. But things were not good in Ireland. The potato crops were poor, and people suffered. When Ernest was six, his landowner father decided to begin a new life. He applied to study medicine at the university in Dublin, and the family left behind country life for the city.

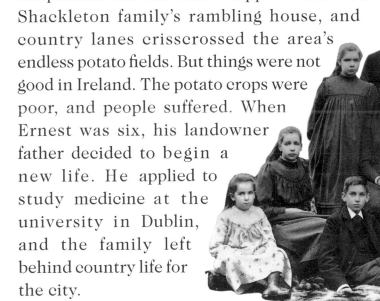

Towering above his brother and eight sisters, Ernest stands at the center of a family portrait. Dressed for one of his early Antarctic expeditions (left), Shackleton wears his polar "helmet" and tunic.

After Ernest's father became a doctor, the family moved from Ireland to England and settled in a London suburb called Sydenham. Ernest, the older son in the big Shackleton family of two boys and eight girls, was good-natured and adored by his sisters. Even though school bored him and he was quick to join in a schoolyard brawl,

Ernest loved to read, and he had a vivid imagination. He attended a secondary school called Dulwich College where a publication later described him as a "rather odd boy who, in spite of an adventurous nature and the spirit of romance that was in him, loved a book better than a bat, solitude better than a crowd, his own companionship better than a mob of other lads...."

Probably it was his love of both adventure and solitude that made him long to go to sea. He had read Jules Verne's *20,000 Leagues Under the Sea,* and he could imagine himself as Captain Nemo, commander of the *Nautilus* submarine. His father, on the other hand, hoped that Ernest would follow him into medicine. But in the end, Dr. Shackleton agreed to let his son go to sea. With ten children to raise, the doctor could not afford the cost of training Ernest as a naval cadet. Instead, he arranged for his son to sign on with a commercial sailing ship bound for South America. Ernest was 16.

Life on board a tall square-rigger meant hard work. Ernest had to climb high up in the ship's rigging to work the sails, even in bad weather and churning waves. "How would you like to be 150 feet up in the air; hanging on with one hand to a rope while with the other you try and get the sail in," Ernest wrote to a friend.

Despite the hardships and months at sea, Ernest loved the life of a merchant marine, a sailor on cargo ships. He also loved poetry and would often recite lines from Robert Browning, his favorite poet, to his shipmates. "When he wasn't on duty on the deck he was stowed away in his cabin with his books," a shipmate remembered.

Ernest spent ten years as a merchant marine. He advanced quickly through the ranks, and by the time he was 24, he was qualified to command a British ship anywhere in the world. When he was on leave, he would come home to visit his family in the London suburbs. On one trip home in 1900, he heard about something called the National Antarctic Expedition. It was being organized by the Royal Geographical Society. The society had sent explorers to Africa and other parts of the globe, and now it wanted to send them to Antarctica.

Few people had ever seen that frigid, forbidding continent of ice, much less explored very far beyond its coastline. But the year before, a Norwegian named Carsten Borchgrevink had spent the winter in Antarctica and gone farther inland than anyone before him.

As an adult, Shackleton usually looked serious and unsmiling in pictures, but he was really a charming man who loved practical jokes. A boyhood picture of him at school (left) shows him wearing a faint smile. At 16 he left school to become a sailor.

The idea of exploring one the of world's last frontiers appealed to Ernest's imagination, and he applied to join the expedition. It would be led by Robert Falcon Scott, a young naval officer. In March 1901 his application was accepted. On the last day of July 1901, the expedition's ship, *Discovery*, sailed down England's River Thames with the 27-year-old Shackleton on board. By early January she had reached the southern seas that swirl around the white continent. Even though it was midsummer in the Southern Hemisphere, huge stretches of pack

"There is something curiously human about the manner and movement of these birds."

ice formed a dangerous floating belt around Antarctica. The sound of the ocean dashing against the ice floes, pushing them into one another, created a groaning that could be heard from far away. No noises of civilization broke the sounds of the polar wild: the roaring sea, the blowing hiss of whales, the squawking penguins and barking seals.

Scott was heading *Discovery* for the Ross Sea, and he had to thread carefully through the pack ice to get there. By January 9 the expedition was closing in on Antarctica, and the snow-clad continent's Admiralty Mountains were visible, rising from Cape Adare. Scott ordered a small landing party to go ashore, and Shackleton was one of the expedition's first members to stand on the shaly Antarctic ground. That ground was slick and foul smelling. Like almost any piece of ice-free land in Antarctica, it was inhabited by thousands of penguins who laid their eggs and raised their young there.

From Cape Adare *Discovery* continued south, passing under the frozen flanks of Mount Erebus, a volcano spouting a plume of smoke. Behind Erebus lay the Ross Ice Shelf, a floating field of ice as big as the state of Texas and as much as 2,000 feet thick.

Huge colonies of penguins live in Antarctica, and the young, like these emperor penguins, often huddle together in rookeries of thousands of birds. Although penguins can't fly in air, they seem to fly through the water. At left, an Adélie uses an icy ledge to launch itself for a deep dive.

Hoping to chart the unexplored coast of the Ross Sea, Scott followed the shoreline west, but *Discovery* was soon surrounded by pack ice and bergs. If the ship were to become trapped by sea ice, it could easily be crushed.

Although no one on board had much experience in polar seas, the crew managed to navigate *Discovery* through the ice safely. But it was clear she could not escape before the pack ice closed and froze her in for the season. The men of the National Antarctic Expedition would have to spend a long winter in the Antarctic. In those days there were no radios or computers to keep ships in touch with the rest of the world. *Discovery* and her men would be on their own.

Scott headed the ship for McMurdo Sound, a well-protected natural harbor on the Antarctic coast. The expedition would winter there. Then, when the brief southern summer came again, they would make a dash overland for the South Pole. Scott and the Royal Geographical Society wanted to plant the British flag at the southernmost spot on the globe.

Despite their hardiness and determination, the British team did not have the kind of equipment they needed for a race to the pole. Other polar pioneers, particularly the Norwegians who had explored the North Pole regions, had found that glacial ice and snow were best tackled on skis, with sleds and teams of dogs to haul equipment. The British had brought skis and dogs with them, but no one on the expedition was an expert with either. After trying unsuccessfully to control the sled dogs and learn to ski, they gave up. They decided instead to walk across the enormous frigid land.

After the British had been at McMurdo for 11 days, Scott appointed Shackleton commander of a three-man expedition to find a good route to start toward the Pole. Pulling a sled loaded with food and gear, Shackleton and his two

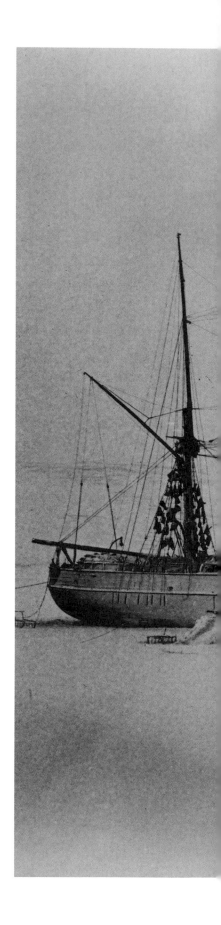

Winter darkness and pack ice surround Discovery, *the ship Shackleton sailed on to Antarctica when he was 27. Trapped by ice,* Discovery *stayed in Antarctica a year longer than planned.*

companions set out. Soon a gale began to blow. Antarctica is actually a desert and hardly ever receives any new precipitation, but winds whip old surface snow into driving blizzards. Now Shackleton and his men bent into the storm with all their might. At night they slept, wet and frozen, huddled together in a small tent. By day they struggled across the Ross Ice Shelf. One misstep could have plunged them to disaster, since a light dusting of snow often hid unseen crevasses—wide, deep cracks in glaciers—where a man could fall to his death.

"It is a unique sort of feeling to look on lands that have never been seen by human eyes before."

Shackleton's goal was a small outcropping of rock sticking up from the ice shelf. He made it there and back to McMurdo in four days. His short expedition didn't really accomplish much, but it did give him a taste for leadership. He found that he had a talent for commanding men, that they would trust their survival to him.

The problem was that Robert Scott, not Shackleton, was the commander of the expedition. Scott, too, could sense that Shackleton was a natural leader, and a rivalry began to grow between the two men. The long, dark months to come would only make it worse.

No sunshine reaches the Antarctic during the depths of winter, and the days passed without a glimmer of light. Other problems also plagued the men, particularly the fear of a disease called scurvy. It causes swollen gums and joints and keeps cuts from healing. After a while, it can lead to mental confusion and death.

Though its cause was then unknown, some scientists believed scurvy came from a lack of fresh food. (They were right. Scientists

Early in the Discovery *expedition a few men, including Shackleton, inflated a hot-air balloon and made the first Antarctic balloon flight. Below,* Discovery *is caught by ice, while open water lies nearby.*

now know that scurvy is caused by a lack of Vitamin C, found in fresh food.) Shackleton wanted Scott to feed the expedition seal meat, as seals were easy to find and would serve as a fresh food source. Scott did not like the idea and wanted to stick with the canned food the expedition had brought along. When some men began showing signs of scurvy, Scott finally agreed to change the diet.

As the daylight slowly returned and the men began to recover their health, thoughts turned to the race for the Pole. Scott planned to take just one man with him—Dr. Edward Wilson—but Wilson convinced Scott that they should also take Shackleton.

A polar explorer casts a shadow on a pressure ridge that has formed a hill of sheer ice. These huge cracked and jagged chunks of ice are squeezed up as plates of pack ice grind toward each other.

Though the Antarctic summer is blessed with long hours of sunlight, it lasts only a few weeks, and blizzards and wind storms can strike at any time. The three-man team would be racing against time, weather, and the threat of scurvy. Their main food would be "hoosh," a stew made of pemmican (ground dried meat) with hard biscuits crumbled in it.

On November 2 they started. This time they took dogs with them, though none of the three knew how to drive a dog team. They struggled along on foot in the snow. As they pushed forward, they left supplies of food buried along the way for their return trip.

Shackleton.   Capt. Scott.   Wilson.
On arrival at the ship after 3 months Southern Sledge Journey.
Nov. 2. 02 — Feb. 2. 03.

They had unusually good weather for the first month, with few blizzards blowing up to create the blinding whiteouts that would force them to stop and wait. Still, they had covered only 109 miles by the beginning of December. The slow going meant their food was running low, and the dogs began to die of hunger and cold; some had to be killed. Shackleton himself was coughing a lot but still straining hard to pull a heavy sled. Now he and Scott, desperately hungry, cold, and exhausted, did not even pretend to respect each other. They also both had swollen gums, a sign of scurvy. Without fresh food they would only get weaker and sicker.

On Christmas Day both Shackleton and Wilson tried to persuade Scott to turn back. They had been out almost six weeks. It would take them that long to get back to the ship. And they were much too far from the South Pole to reach it. But Scott refused. They kept going forward till December 30. In the afternoon Shackleton stayed with the supplies, while the other two men continued a mile or two farther. They were measuring their progress not so much by miles as by latitude—imaginary lines that circle the globe from the Equator, at 0° latitude, to the Poles. The South Pole is at 90°S, and they had reached latitude 82°17'. That was to be their "Furthest South." Now, at last, Scott agreed to turn around and race for the ship.

It was a race for their lives. Supplies were desperately low, and the health and strength of the men, particularly Shackleton, were failing quickly. Though Shackleton tried to pull his share of the load, he began to cough up blood, and it was hard for him to breathe. Finally, Wilson, the doctor, forced him to stop pulling the sleds and follow on skis. For one afternoon Shackleton was so weak he had to ride on a sled. The humiliation of that would haunt him all his life.

After their race toward the South Pole in the winter of 1902, Shackleton, Robert Scott, and Dr. Edward Wilson returned to camp. They had traveled 200 miles farther south than any people before them, but that was still 450 miles short of the Pole.

Return of the Southern
Sledge. party.
Feb. 2. 1903.

Capt. Scott

E. a. Wilson.

Cross.

Skelton

Bernacchi

Armitage.

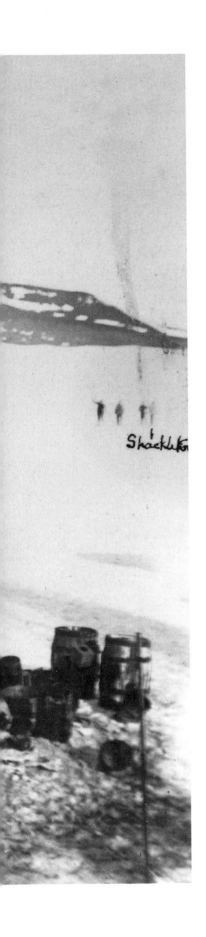

Shackleton

"What a little speck on the snowy wilderness is our camp, all round white... and the sun shining down on it all."

On their last legs, the men got help from the wind. Roaring at their backs, it blew them across the barren Antarctic snows, and they made it to *Discovery* on February 3. One of the crew members described how strange the three men looked with their "long beards, hair, dirt, swollen lips & peeled complexions, & blood-shot eyes...." The expedition was a disappointment. They had not succeeded in getting very close to the Pole, and they had come very close to losing their lives.

Shackleton's own sense of failure deepened when Scott ordered him home on a relief ship that had sailed into the open waters of McMurdo Sound, four miles away from the British base. *Discovery,* still locked in ice, would have to remain yet another year, until the ice melted the following austral, or southern, summer. Shackleton argued to stay, but Scott would not allow it. Officially, Scott wrote that he was ordering Shackleton's return "solely on account of his health." But Scott also resented Shackleton and his natural ability as a leader. From that time on, the two men would be rivals in a lifelong race to best each other at the Pole.

Straggling into camp after their three-month ordeal on the ice, Scott, Wilson, and Shackleton were met by shipmates relieved to see them safe. Shackleton, bringing up the rear, was suffering from scurvy and a weak heart.

"Never mind my beloved whether the days are dull or cold or dark, we will be all brightness and light in our little house...."

When the disappointed Shackleton returned to England in 1903 at the age of 29, his longtime sweetheart, Emily Dorman, was waiting for him. She was a friend of his sisters whom he had met on leave when he was still a sailor. For several years he had been pouring his heart out to her in letters, telling her his thoughts and dreams. Emily understood Shackleton and his restless spirit well, saying about him, "One must not chain down an eagle in a barnyard." In April 1904 the two were married and soon settled in Edinburgh, Scotland, where Shackleton was running the offices of the Royal Scottish Geographical Society. With his usual charm and energy, Shackleton stormed through the society, making changes and exerting his natural influence as a leader. But after about a year, he found the work tedious, and he longed for something more exciting.

That would be the pattern of his life. He tried journalism, running for Parliament, and a number of exotic—and questionable—financial investments that he hoped would make him rich. But life in Britain never quite suited the adventuresome Anglo-Irishman. Ernest was simply bored by routine. And that lonely, windswept desert of ice and snow at the bottom of the world always called to him.

By 1907 Shackleton was deep in plans for his own expedition to the Pole. With the help

After a long courtship, Shackleton married Emily Dorman. Six years older than he was, Emily was always patient with his dreams. When their first child, Raymond (right), was born in 1905, Shackleton was said to have declared the baby had "good fists for fighting!"

of friends and admirers, he pieced together the money needed to fund it. When Scott learned of the plans, he made Shackleton promise not to land at McMurdo Sound, claiming that part of the frozen continent for himself. No one had any claim to the continent, and Scott's request was unreasonable, but Shackleton reluctantly agreed to it.

The expedition ship, *Nimrod,* was a 41-year-old sealer from Newfoundland—not exactly the perfect vessel to take into the stormy southern oceans, but Shackleton, as always, was determined. Instead of the sled dogs he had found so troublesome on his previous polar expedition, he was taking small Manchurian ponies for transport, and a new invention, a motor car! As he sailed south, he wrote to Emily, "It gives me a lump in my throat when I think of my family."

By mid-January 1908 *Nimrod* was edging along the Antarctic coast, looking for a place on the Ross Ice Shelf called Barrier Inlet. But the inlet was gone! The ice that had formed it had calved, or broken away, from

Hauled up on the ice Probably to sun itself, a seal seems more interested in the photographer taking its picture than in the contraption behind it—a Scottish motor car donated to the expedition. It proved useless on the ice.

the main ice shelf and floated out to sea. The discovery shocked Shackleton, and he decided not to chance making a base on or near the unstable edge of the ice barrier. He began searching for another safe landing spot, but he couldn't locate one. With no other choice, he headed *Nimrod* for McMurdo Sound. He would not risk the lives of his men to keep his promise to Scott. He wrote to his wife about his decision, saying, "My conscience is clear but my heart is sore...."

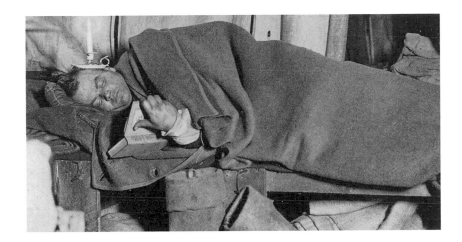

Tucked into his bunk on Nimrod, George Marston, the expedition's artist, reads by the light of a carefully balanced candle. Like many others on Nimrod, Marston would follow Shackleton to Antarctica again aboard Endurance.

At McMurdo Sound the expedition planned to set up a base at Hut Point, Scott's old camp. But pack ice blocked them. So they set up a base at nearby Cape Royds. They tried using the car to transfer supplies, but its tires could not get a good grip on the drifting snow. Once unloaded, *Nimrod* sailed back to New Zealand with orders to return in February 1909. For the next year the 13 men of the expedition would be on their own and out of contact with the rest of the world. They built a small hut, their only shelter from the weather, and settled in. Always concerned about keeping his men's spirits up, Shackleton ordered a small expedition to climb 12,448-foot Mount Erebus, where no human had set foot before. On March 10, after a five-day struggle, five men made it to the top. But winter was now closing in. Cramped together in the hut, the men talked, slept away the endless, tedious days, longed for home, and made plans for the run to the Pole.

Shackleton planned to take three men with him—Jameson Adams, Dr. Eric Marshall, and Frank Wild. In late August, when weak sunlight finally broke the endless Antarctic winter night, the men began laying in supplies at Hut Point, 20 miles away.

Shackleton's Burberry "helmet" was inscribed by him to say, in part, that it was not meant for "when knights were bold," but for "when nights were cold." To keep spirits up during the long winter days at the McMurdo Sound camp, Shackleton sent a small group to the summit of Mount Erebus, where they looked into its volcanic crater (left).

"At last we are out on the long trail after 4 years thought and work."

At last, on October 29 with a bright sun shining in the blue polar sky, the adventure began. Since the car had failed, they used ponies to haul gear. The South Pole was about 750 treacherous miles away, and they had enough food for 91 days. That meant they had to cover an average of 16 miles a day—on foot.

After less than two weeks, the men realized the ponies were no good as polar pack animals. They could not stand the cold, and their heavy weight broke through the snow, sometimes sending them plunging down crevasses. In the end, all of the ponies died. Their carcasses provided the men with much-needed fresh meat to ward off scurvy. Once again Shackleton found himself and his men pulling heavy sleds toward the South Pole.

Shackleton had hoped that a vast plain of snow and ice lay between him and his goal. But he was wrong. The high, jagged Transantarctic Mountains stood in his path. But luck was on his side. In early December he and his men came upon one of the few passes through the mountains. A glacier they called the Golden Gateway led them to a stupendous

ice field 30 miles wide and more than 100 miles long. Wild believed that it "must be the largest in the world...." Though deep snow, crevasses, and other obstacles marred its glistening blue surface, still it beckoned like a wide road, and Shackleton and his men took it.

A week later they were still climbing the glacier, scrambling over high ridges of ice, roped together to keep from falling into hidden crevasses. As they climbed higher, the cold and wind grew worse, and frostbite threatened their fingers, toes, and faces. They were running low on food and had little fuel left either to cook with or to melt snow for drinking water. Yet they kept going, and by December 28 they at last left the glacier behind and became the first humans ever to set foot on the smooth, vast ice cap that covers the South Pole.

With each passing day, cold and hunger gnawed at them. Shackleton now had to admit that he would not reach the Pole itself, but he was determined to get within a hundred miles of it. Finally, on January 9, Marshall, the expedition navigator, calculated that they were at 88°23' south, about 97 miles from the Pole. They had beaten Scott's Furthest South—by 360 miles!

Shackleton agreed now to turn around, but hundreds of miles lay between the men and the safety of Hut Point. Along the way, they had to locate the food depots that they had left for their return trip.

None of the ponies Shackleton used for his 1908 race to the Pole survived. They sank into the snow instead of gliding on it, and they were always cold and hungry. Shackleton and his men spent valuable hours caring for them.

At one point, they had nothing to eat for 40 hours. They were in a race to survive.

While the four men were struggling toward Hut Point, *Nimrod* had returned to McMurdo Sound. The captain had orders to wait for Shackleton and his men until March 1. After that, he should consider them lost and sail back to New Zealand. On February 28, as the ship waited, everyone on board believed that the men had died. Then, on March 1, they spotted two tiny figures waving a flag at Hut Point. It was Shackleton and Wild! They had struggled ahead to make it in time.

Once again Shackleton had failed to reach the Pole, but to Emily he wrote, "Though I may be disappointed I will come back to the loving arms...of you my wife and in the joy of seeing you...and our children all will be forgotten." And once again, too, he had proved his leadership. All his men returned to England safely, and Shackleton was hailed as a hero. To honor him as a great adventurer of the age, King Edward VII knighted him Sir Ernest Shackleton.

Four men from Nimrod (left to right)—
Frank Wild, Shackleton, Eric Marshall, and
Jameson Adams—set a new "Furthest South"
record, coming within 97 miles of the Pole.

On December 14, 1911, a Norwegian party (top), led by famous polar explorer Roald Amundsen, won the race to the South Pole. At the same time, Robert Scott (below, center, standing), was leading his own polar expedition. All five men on it perished.

The very next year a Norwegian party led by Roald Amundsen did what Shackleton had failed to do. On December 14, 1911, they reached the South Pole. Although Shackleton had lost the race to the Pole, he was still haunted by the Antarctic world. Now 39 years old, he began planning a third expedition to Antarctica. He had a new goal: to cross the entire continent, a journey of 1,500 miles. This would mean using two ships. One group would go with him to the Weddell Sea. Shackleton named this ship, a Norwegian polar ship, *Endurance,* after his family motto: "By endurance we conquer."

On the way south to Antarctica in 1914, Endurance *put in at the whaling station on South Georgia Island to buy provisions. Frank Hurley, the expedition's photographer, persuaded a few shipmates to help him lug his heavy camera gear up a mountaintop for a shot down on* Endurance *at anchor in the harbor. Little did the men know what role the island would eventually play in their fate.*

After landing, they would make the overland crossing in what Shackleton hoped would be a hundred days. This time he would use sled dogs. Meanwhile, a second ship, *Aurora,* would sail to the Ross Sea at the opposite side of the continent. A land party from the ship would lay supply depots a hundred miles into the interior so that Shackleton and his party would have food when they neared the far side of the continent. Once they reached the coast of the Ross Sea, *Aurora* would pick them up.

Just as the two ships sailed from Europe in 1914, fighting broke out between England and Germany. The First World War had begun. The men aboard *Endurance* had no idea how much this would change the world they were leaving behind.

As always, the two Antarctic-bound ships planned to arrive at their destinations during the austral summer so they would have time to establish bases before winter set in. But when *Endurance* neared the continent in mid-December, unseasonable pack ice forced her to push her way slowly through the Weddell Sea. On January 19 the sound of the battering suddenly stopped. *Endurance* was caught by the ice and held tight. Around her the sea was frozen in every direction as far as the eye could see. The ship was only a day's sail from the landing base Shackleton had been aiming for, but now he was helpless. He had no choice but to drift with the pack.

Dwarfed by an iceberg, Endurance *used steam power to thread her way through the ice. Built for polar seas, the 144-foot-long ship could shove through loose ice, "shattering the floes in grand style."*

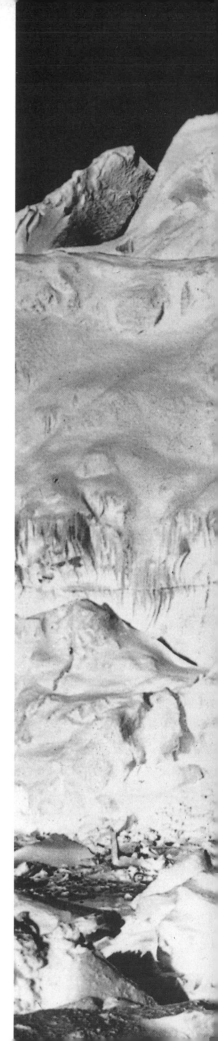

"Pack-ice might be described as a gigantic and interminable jigsaw puzzle devised by nature."

After almost a month of being helplessly frozen in, the men saw a gash of open water just a few hundred yards from the ship. Shackleton sent a group out with saws to try to hack a channel in the ice from the ship to the open water. They sawed away, but in places the ice was 18 feet thick. The job was impossible. Although open water was close, they could not get *Endurance* to it. They would have to wait for the ice to break up on its own.

By March, winter was setting in. The currents and winds changed back and forth, sometimes pushing them south toward Antarctica, and sometimes pushing them away from the continent and into unknown seas. Through it all, Shackleton remained the calm, cheerful leader who was affectionately called "Boss" by his men.

Working frantically, the men tried to cut a lead through the ice for Endurance *(left). Warmed by the ship's stove, shipmates keep the night watchman company.*

To pass the long, boring days, the 29 men aboard *Endurance* played parlor games like, animal, vegetable, mineral, or they impersonated one another or sang songs.

In early August the pack ice at last began to break up. But Shackleton and a few others realized that, far from escape, this might mean the death of *Endurance*. Frozen in place the ship was safe, but now the

A stowaway who became ship steward, 19-year-old Perce Blackborow poses with the expedition's cat, Mrs. Chippy. Angry that Blackborow had snuck aboard his ship, Shackleton gruffly told the young sailor, "the first person we eat will be you." Leonard Hussey (far left) hoists sled dog Samson. At times the men played soccer on the frozen pack ice that held Endurance fast.

grinding, unstable pressure ridges of ice, which looked like frozen waves, could squeeze the ship. By late October *Endurance* was caught in a vise of ice that buckled her seams and allowed the frigid ocean water to seep in. The men fought hard to save her by pumping out the water, but it was no good. On October 27 her timbers creaked and groaned, and her beams cracked.

"What the ice takes, the ice keeps."

"It was a pitiful sight," one expedition member wrote. "To all of us she seemed like a living thing...and it was awful to witness her torture."

Shackleton ordered the men to abandon ship, move their gear out onto an ice floe, and set up tents for shelter. Now they were shipless, floating they knew not where on an enormous moving island of ice, and no one in the world knew where they were.

Shackleton never believed in giving up. Soon the Boss had a plan. The men would march 312 miles across the floes to an old Swedish base at Snow Hill, where there would probably be some supplies. From there, Shackleton would take a small party another 130 miles overland to Wilhelmina Bay, a place whalers often patrolled. But his plan had a problem. The floe ice was mushy, and the men sank in with every step. Hauling heavy sleds full of gear was almost impossible.

Sled dogs watch as Endurance *is crushed by ice. "She was doomed: no ship built by human hands could have withstood the strain," Shackleton wrote. Hauling lifeboats and sleds over pack ice, the men tried to reach a hut 312 miles away, but the going was too hard.*

"Living in a tent without any furniture requires a little getting used to."

After a while, they stopped trying and set up a base they called Ocean Camp. It was November 1, 1915.

To ward off scurvy, the men hunted seal and penguin for food. They used blubber—fat from the seals—as fuel for cooking and to melt ice for drinking water. In the evenings they played cards and sang to keep their spirits up.

In late December the pack ice began to break up, and Shackleton moved camp. But again the going was very tough, and the men did not get far before settling onto another floe they called Patience Camp.

Shackleton (left) and Frank Wild survey the scene at Ocean Camp, where the men spent two months. Set up on pack ice about a mile and a half from the wreck of Endurance, the camp's location allowed the men to go back to the ship and salvage supplies from it.

The ice was being blown east then west by the winds and currents, and the men could do nothing but wait. By late March 1916, after five months on the ice, their camp floe was getting dangerously thin.

Then suddenly, they spotted land in the distance. It was Joinville Island, at the tip of the Antarctic Peninsula. But they couldn't reach it, and they now realized that they were being swept out of the Weddell Sea into the open ocean. Their floe had shrunk to a small island only big enough for their camp. And it was beginning to disintegrate beneath their feet. On April 9 Shackleton knew they had to abandon the floe. They crowded into three boats they had dragged with them from *Endurance* and set out on the stormy southern seas.

Weaving through drifting pack ice, they rowed and sailed all day, then pulled up on a long floe at night to rest. About 11 p.m. Shackleton felt uneasy and got up to check on things. As he walked across the floe, the ice suddenly cracked under his feet and ran under a tent up ahead, tipping a man in his sleeping bag into the frigid water. Shackleton quickly pulled him back onto the floe, just before the crack snapped shut again! The man struggled out of his bag, "wet but otherwise unscathed." No one slept the rest of that night.

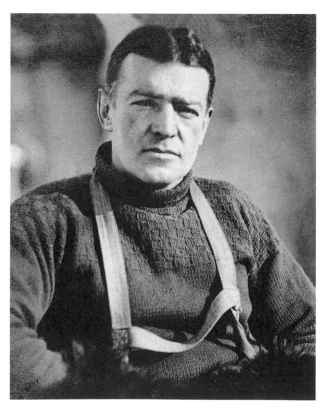

The next day, it was back in the boats. And the next and the next and the next. Waves sent freezing water hurling over the men, turning their clothes to ice. They were always wet and cold, and the rough waters often made them seasick. They had no drinking water, so they were forever thirsty. They didn't know when— or if—they would sight land again.

When Endurance *went down, Shackleton (left) said to his men, "Ship and stores have gone—so now we'll go home." Despite the desperate situation, the men never lost faith in his leadership. A diary (right) shows some of their gear, including finneskos— Lapp shoes made of reindeer hide.*

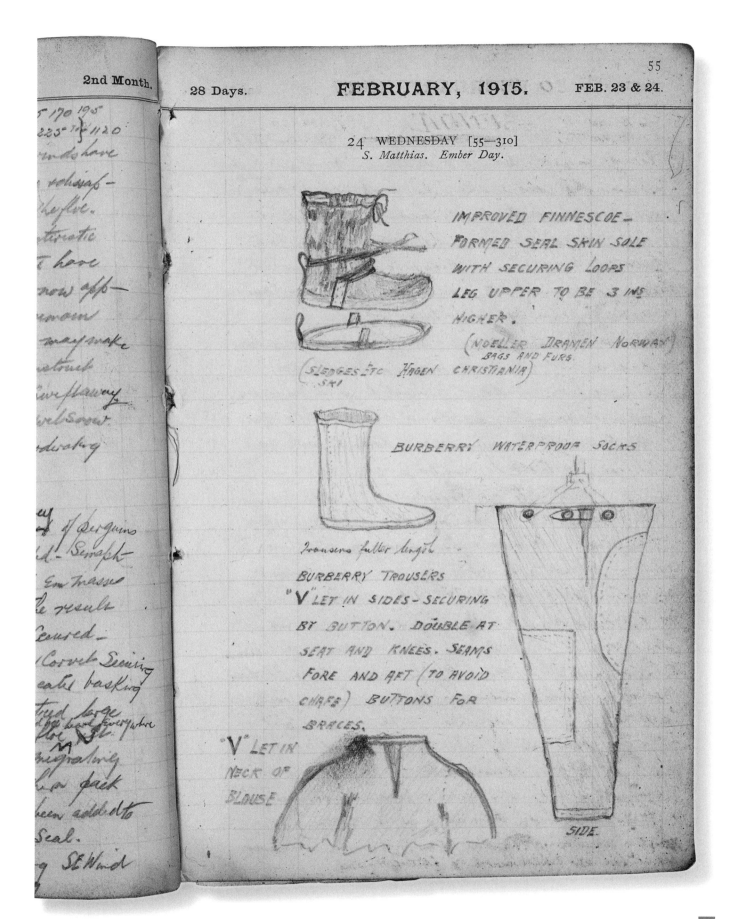

24 WEDNESDAY [55—310]
S. Matthias. Ember Day.

IMPROVED FINNESCOE-
FORMED SEAL SKIN SOLE
WITH SECURING LOOPS
LEG UPPER TO BE 3 INS
HIGHER.
(NOELLER DRAMEN NORWAY)
BAGS AND FURS.
(SLEDGES ETC HAGEN CHRISTIANIA)
SKI

BURBERRY WATERPROOF SOCKS

Trousers fuller length
BURBERRY TROUSERS
"V" LET IN SIDES - SECURING
BY BUTTON. DOUBLE AT
SEAT AND KNEES. SEAMS
FORE AND AFT (TO AVOID
CHAFE) BUTTONS FOR
BRACES.

"V" LET IN
NECK OF
BLOUSE

SIDE.

Then, after six days, they saw land ahead! It was Elephant Island, an uninhabited place with sheer cliffs pounded by waves. At first they could find no landing spot, and for another day they were stuck at sea as they circled the island, looking for a safe place to beach the boats. At last they landed on a narrow, rocky beach. "Conceive our joy on setting foot on solid earth after 170 days of life on a drifting ice floe...," the expedition's photographer, Hurley, wrote. The men heated milk and drank a toast to their success.

Shackleton had brought all his men safely across raging southern seas. Now he had to get them, somehow, back to civilization. He decided his only choice was to cross more ocean. A whaling station run by Norwegians lay on the island of South Georgia, more than 700 treacherous miles away. It was a small dot in the vast sea. But he would have to sail there.

After a harrowing ocean crossing, the men reached uninhabited Elephant Island. In his picture of the landing (below), photographer Hurley drew an iceberg in the background. For four months, 22 men lived on the island in a hut roofed by two overturned boats.

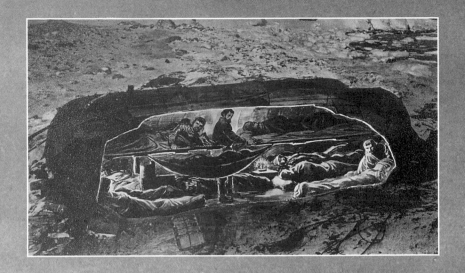

"The men who were staying behind made a pathetic little group on the beach, with...the sea seething at their feet...."

On April 24, a week after the group had arrived on Elephant Island, Shackleton and five other men pushed off in the 22-foot-long *James Caird*. Of all the hardships they had already managed to survive, they knew this journey would be their toughest challenge. And it was. Gales blew against them, and ice caked on them and on the canvas sheet that covered part of their boat. They took turns sleeping, a few at a time crawling into the narrow bow space under the canvas, where reindeer hair from their sleeping bags got into their noses and eyes. Heavy seas broke their anchor line, so they could not stop. At one point a wave as high as a four-story building broke over the boat, and the men bailed frantically to keep from sinking. And all the while, they worried that they might sweep past South Georgia without ever seeing it and be lost in the endless ocean.

As Shackleton and five others set out again in the James Caird *(above), the men left on Elephant Island waved a hearty farewell. "The* Caird *is an excellent sailer, &...should make Sth. Georgia in 14 days," Hurley predicted. It took 17 days "of supreme strife," Shackleton later wrote.*

"The mountains peered through the mists, and between them huge glaciers poured down the great ice-slopes which lay behind."

But their navigator, Worsley, somehow managed to keep them on track. And, just after noon on May 8, there it was! The very island they had been aiming for. But just as at Elephant Island, surf pounded against mean, steep cliffs, making landing impossible. To make matters worse, a hurricane was shrieking in on top of them. So, with land in view and their thirst parching them, they had to wait. Finally, after two days of struggling against the weather and searching for a landing spot, they beached the *James Caird* in a small cove. But the ordeal was not over. The whaling station lay on the far side of the island. They had to cross the mountains and glaciers that covered the interior of South Georgia.

After resting for a few days, Shackleton, Frank Worsley, and Thomas Crean made a dash for the far side of the island. They took no sleeping bags, and each man carried his food in three socks tied around his neck so his hands would be free to climb. Several times as they labored up and down the snow-clad mountains, they got lost and had to retrace their steps, even though they were bone tired. On one steep snowy slope, the men took a chance and slid down.

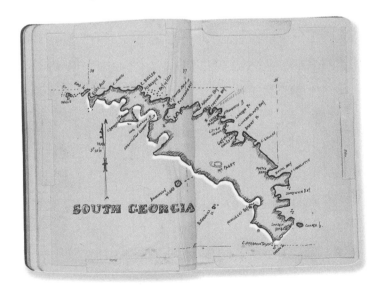

"Savage and horrible," the world-navigating explorer Captain James Cook called South Georgia 140 years before Shackleton arrived. A rough map shows names dotting the coast but none in the snow-swept mountainous interior.

"For a moment my hair stood on end," Worsley later wrote. "Then...quite suddenly...I was actually enjoying it." So were Shackleton and Crean.

Finally, after more than 24 hours of constant climbing and their strength failing them, they spotted the whaling station below. Hurrying in that direction, they found a waterfall in their way. But they weren't going to be slowed now. They slid down it using a rope, as they had slid down the snow slope, and kept walking. Their "dash" had taken 36 hours, but now help was really at hand.

They straggled into the whaling station looking like wild men, their

eyes bloodshot, their faces burned dark by wind, sun, and soot from blubber fires. Two little boys saw them and ran away, frightened. The boss of the whaling station had known Shackleton before and recognized his voice. He welcomed them and fed them breads, cakes, and other treats they had not had for more than a year and a half.

At the Grytviken whaling station on South Georgia, Norwegian workers begin to flense—or strip blubber from—a whale. The stench of whale flesh filled the air in these stations, all of which are now closed.

"We had pierced the veneer of outside things. We had suffered, starved and triumphed...."

As nice as it was to be back in civilization, Shackleton was anxious to rescue his men. That same night the station boss sent a boat to pick up the men on the other side of South Georgia. That part was easy, but it would be a long, hard struggle to get the men back from Elephant Island.

Shackleton tried four times in four different boats to get through the pack ice around the island. The fourth time he finally made it in a Chilean ship called *Yelcho*. It was August 28, 1916. It had been 126 days since Shackleton had set sail in *James Caird*, and the men left on the island were beginning to lose hope.

Despite all the months of cold, hunger, and wet, not a single man had been lost. When his wife, Emily, heard that he and his men were safe, she said, "I am so thankful that he rescued his men...instead of being *fetched*."

A newspaper picture shows a beaming Emily Shackleton and her two youngest children, Cecily and Edward, after she learns that her husband is safe. For more than a year, the family had not known if he were alive or dead.

LADY SHACKLETON LEARNS WITH JOY THAT HER HUSBAND IS SAFE.

Lady Shackleton and two of her children walking through the Park yesterday.

"A curious piece of ice on the horizon…bore a striking resemblance to a ship," one of the men on Elephant Island recalled, as the Chilean ship Yelcho came within sight. The men lit a fire to attract the ship's attention, and soon Shackleton was rowing ashore to rescue them.

"Sometimes I think I am no good at anything but being away in the wilds...."

But there was one more rescue to be made before Shackleton could rest. The group of men from the ship *Aurora* had been stranded for more than two years at McMurdo Sound while *Aurora itself was* stuck in Australia, plagued by weather and financial problems. Shackleton now had to sail halfway around the world to Australia and then take *Aurora* to Antarctica. When he picked up the survivors, he found that two of the men were missing, and one had died. Though Shackleton searched for the missing men for days, he found no trace of them.

When at last Shackleton returned home to England and his wife and children, the First World War was still raging. He wanted to do his part, and for a while he helped organize troops and supplies amid the arctic cold of northern Russia. But when the war was over, he was once again bored with everyday life. He began planning another expedition, this one to circle the entire Antarctic continent by ship. Many of the men from *Endurance* wanted to go with him. To them, he was forever the Boss—the greatest leader and hero they had ever known.

In December 1921 they steamed south once again, and by early January their ship, *Quest,* was in South Georgia. But Shackleton's health was failing. Since his very first expedition with Scott, he had suspected that he had a weak heart. Now, at last, it gave out. On January 5, 1922, the Boss died. He was 47 years old. "We would have gone anywhere without question just on his order...," one of his men wrote. "Now that he is gone, there is a gap in our lives that can never be filled."

His wife, Emily, decided that her husband should be buried on South Georgia, and that is where Shackleton lies today—amid the wild glaciers and roaring gales of the southern lands he loved so well.

Aboard Quest, *Shackleton made the final journey of his life—back to the Antarctic. Revisiting the whaling station on South Georgia, he regained some of his old enthusiasm, though in his diary he confessed, "I grow old and tired but must always lead on."*

The men aboard Quest left their picture and signatures buried in a bottle at the foot of Shackleton's grave on South Georgia. Many of them had been with the Boss on Endurance as well, and to them he was the leader they would never forget. Their "message in a bottle" was discovered only in recent years.

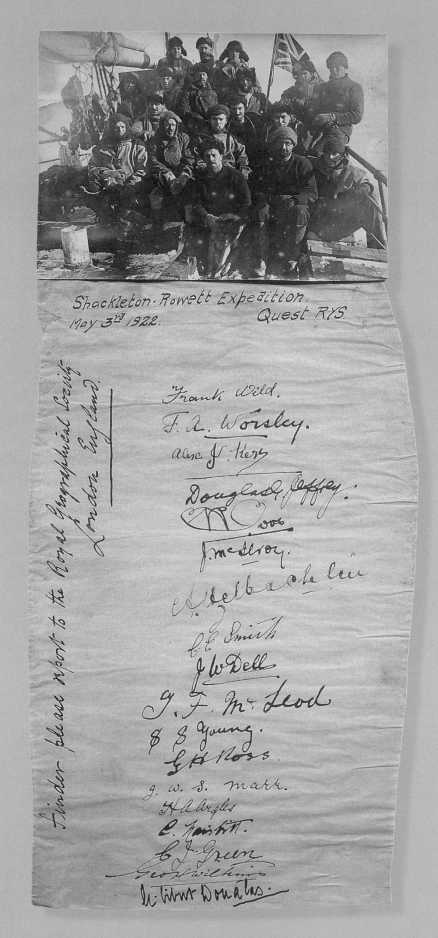

Shackleton-Rowett Expedition.
May 3rd 1922.   Quest RYS.

Finder please report to the Royal Geographical Society London England.

Frank Wild.
F. A. Worsley.
Alex J. Kerr
Douglas Jeffrey.
J. McIlroy.
A. Helbach lin
C. C. Smith
J. W. Dell
G. F. McLeod
S. S. Young.
G. H. Ross.
J. W. S. Marr.
H. A. Argles
C. Naisbitt.
C. J. Green
Geo. Wilkins
Wilbur Douglas.

AFTERWORD

RNEST SHACKLETON NEVER STOOD AT THE SOUTH POLE. HE NEVER circumnavigated Antarctica. He never achieved the goals he set for himself. He lived not quite 48 years and died exhausted, dispirited, and in debt. Yet he always followed his dreams. "I shall go on going...till one day I shall not come back," he said near the end of his life. Like many people whose accomplishments have won them lasting fame and admiration, Shackleton did not realize what he had contributed to humankind.

Yet now he is considered one of the greatest explorers and natural leaders the world has ever known. His name has become so synonymous with bravery and endurance that when other explorers set out on their own quests, they sometimes simply say the name—Shackleton—to give them courage. Even today, the story of *Endurance* is one of the world's great tales of adventure. Most people, finding themselves helplessly adrift on ice at the end of the Earth, would simply give up. But not Shackleton. "Never the lowered Banner/Never the lost Endeavor," he proclaimed. His calm confidence, unfailing optimism, and selfless leadership inspired his men to believe that they all could—and would—survive.

Surviving against the odds was his talent, and he preferred the simple ferocity of Antarctica, where the fight for survival was a daily challenge, to the disappointments, intrigues, and routines of the civilized world. "Courage and willpower can make miracles," Shackleton's friend and fellow polar explorer Roald Amundsen said of him, adding, "I know of no better example than what that man has accomplished."

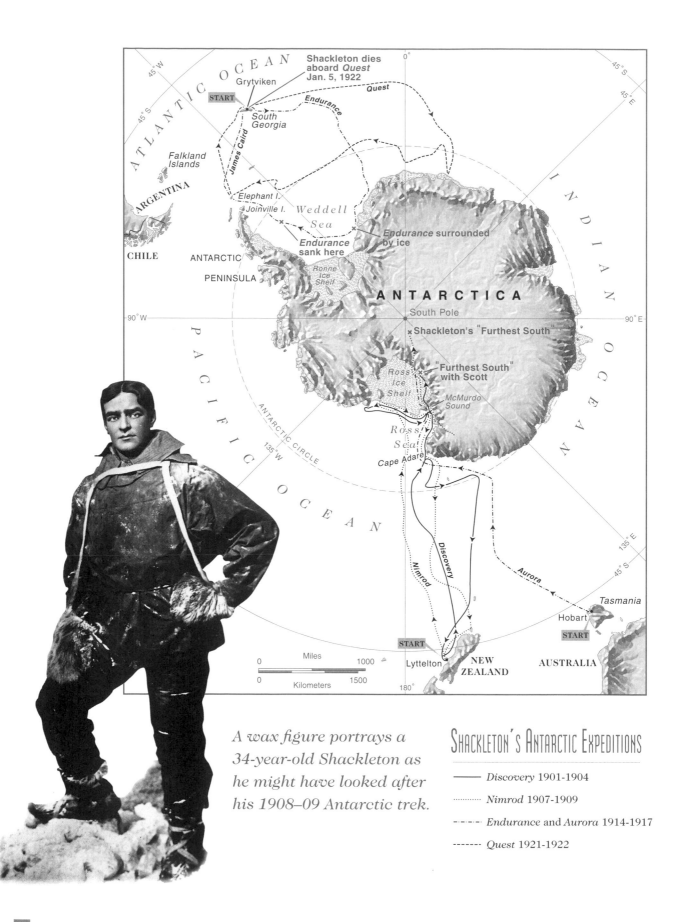

Shackleton dies
aboard *Quest*
Jan. 5, 1922

ATLANTIC OCEAN

Grytviken

START

Quest

Endurance

South
Georgia

James Caird

Falkland
Islands

ARGENTINA

CHILE

Elephant I.

Joinville I.

*Weddell
Sea*

Endurance
sank here

Endurance surrounded
by ice

ANTARCTIC

PENINSULA

*Ronne
Ice
Shelf*

INDIAN OCEAN

ANTARCTICA

South Pole

x Shackleton's "Furthest South"

90° W

90° E

*Ross
Ice
Shelf*

x "Furthest South"
with Scott

*McMurdo
Sound*

PACIFIC OCEAN

*Ross
Sea*

Cape Adare

ANTARCTIC CIRCLE

135° W

Discovery

Nimrod

Aurora

135° E

45° S

Tasmania

Hobart

START

Miles

0   1000

START

Lyttelton

NEW
ZEALAND

AUSTRALIA

0   1500
Kilometers

180°

*A wax figure portrays a
34-year-old Shackleton as
he might have looked after
his 1908–09 Antarctic trek.*

Shackleton's Antarctic Expeditions

——— *Discovery* 1901-1904

············ *Nimrod* 1907-1909

–·–·–· *Endurance* and *Aurora* 1914-1917

------ *Quest* 1921-1922

Chronology

1874	Ernest Henry Shackleton born in County Kildare, Ireland, on February 15
1890	Leaves Dulwich College at the age of 16 and goes to sea
1901	Joins the National Antarctic Expedition headed by Robert Falcon Scott
1902	With Scott and Wilson gets closer to the South Pole than anyone has before
1909	He and three other men get within 97 miles of the South Pole.
1909	Knighted Sir Ernest Shackleton
1911	Norwegian Roald Amundsen becomes the first person to reach the South Pole.
1914	Begins expedition to cross the Antarctic continent *Endurance* sails for Weddell Sea and *Aurora* for McMurdo Sound.
1915	In late January *Endurance* becomes frozen in pack ice. In late November *Endurance,* crushed by the ice, sinks.
1916	In April Shackleton and his men make an open-boat journey to Elephant Island. He and five other men then sail more than 700 miles to reach help on South Georgia.
1917	Rescue of *Aurora* crew stranded at McMurdo Sound
1921	In December Shackleton sails aboard *Quest* on his fourth expedition, intending to circumnavigate Antarctica.
1922	Shackleton dies aboard *Quest* off South Georgia on January 5.

Bibliography

Alexander, Caroline. "Epic of Survival: Shackleton." NATIONAL GEOGRAPHIC (November 1998) 84–101.

Alexander, Caroline. *The Endurance: Shackleton's Legendary Antarctic Expedition.* New York: Alfred A. Knopf, Inc., 1998.

Heacox, Kim. *Shackleton: The Antarctic Challenge.* Washington, D.C.: National Geographic Society, 1999.

Huntford, Roland. *Shackleton.* New York: Atheneum, 1986.

Lansing, Alfred. *Endurance: Shackleton's Incredible Voyage.* New York: Carroll and Graf Publishers, Inc., 1986, 1998.

The world's largest nonprofit scientific and educational organization, the National Geographic Society was founded in 1888 "for the increase and diffusion of geographic knowledge." Since then it has supported scientific exploration and spread information to its more than nine million members worldwide.

The National Geographic Society educates and inspires millions every day through magazines, books, television programs, videos, maps and atlases, research grants, the National Geography Bee, teacher workshops, and innovative classroom materials.

The Society is supported through membership dues and income from the sale of its educational products. Members receive NATIONAL GEOGRAPHIC magazine — the Society's official journal — discounts on Society products, and other benefits.

For more information about the National Geographic Society and its educational programs and publications, please call 1-800-NGS-LINE (647-5463) or write to the following address:

National Geographic Society
1145 17th Street N.W.
Washington, D.C. 20036-4688 U.S.A.

Visit the Society's Web site:
www.nationalgeographic.com